LON
Ser

# GIRL against the JUNGLE

## Monica Vincent

Illustrations by Steve Noon

Longman

**Longman Group UK Limited,**
*Longman House, Burnt Mill, Harlow,*
*Essex CM20 2JE, England*
*and Associated Companies throughout the world*

First published 1978 in Longman Structural Readers
This edition first published 1993 in Longman Originals
Fifth impression 1994

Set in 12/14pt Melior, Adobe/Linotype (postscript)

Produced by Longman Singapore Publishers Pte Ltd
Printed in Singapore

ISBN 0 582 07498 3

**Acknowledgements**

The author wishes to thank the London School of
Hygiene and Tropical Medicine for advice in preparing
this book.

We are grateful to Pixfeatures Press Service for their
permission to reproduce copyright photographs on
pages 3 and 30.

## Suzanne at school

(front row, centre)

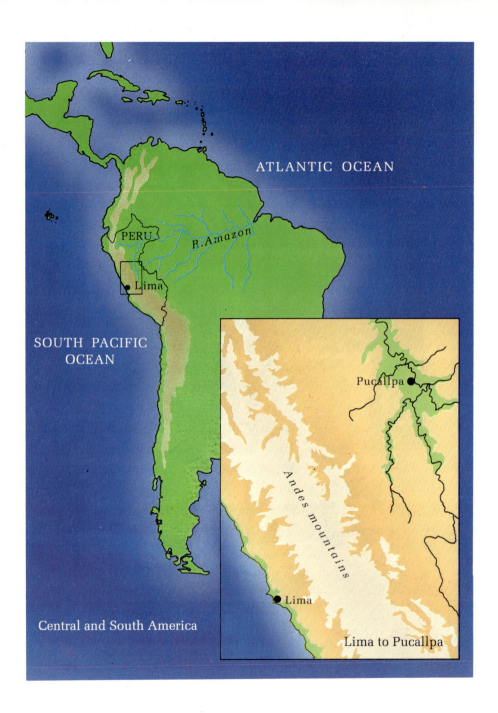

ATLANTIC OCEAN

PERU

R. Amazon

Lima

SOUTH PACIFIC
OCEAN

Pucallpa

Andes mountains

Lima

Central and South America

Lima to Pucallpa

# Girl Against the Jungle

It was Christmas Eve and I was very happy. I was with my mother at Lima Airport.

"Tomorrow will be Christmas Day," I thought, "and I'll be home. I'll be home in the jungle for Christmas."

"Oh, I want to get home quickly," I said. "Why is our plane late?"

"These small planes are often late," said my mother. "But we'll be home for Christmas."

"Has Dad found a Christmas tree?" I asked.

"Yes, he has."

"How's Pépé?"

"He's very well. He often talks about you."

"I bought him a Christmas present in Paris," I said. "I've bought presents for you and Dad, too. But you can't see them today."

My mother smiled. "I can wait another day," she said. "But listen. They're calling our flight now."

I heard the voice from the loudspeaker. "Will passengers for flight number 318 to Pucallpa please go to Gate 5."

"Come on," said my mother. We picked up our cases and hurried to the plane. I found a seat next to a window.

"You sit there," said my mother. "Then you can look out of the window at the jungle. You'll like that. I'm going to read this new book about birds."

I could see the tops of the Andes mountains.

The plane took off and started to climb up into the sky. It climbed up and up. Then it started to fly straight, so I looked out of the window. I could see the tops of the Andes mountains. "I'll see the jungle soon," I thought.

"All right?" asked my mother.

"Yes," I said. "I'm going to like this flight. I haven't seen the jungle for three months."

We flew over the Andes and had a meal. Then I looked out of the window again, but I couldn't see much. It was only 11.30 in the morning but the sky was very dark. I looked for the dark green trees of the jungle but I couldn't see them. I could only see dark clouds. Suddenly the plane jumped and my case fell onto the floor. I tried to pick it up.

"Leave it," said my mother, "and stay in your seat. This isn't going to be an easy flight."

The plane rolled to one side and a passenger screamed. A voice came from the loudspeaker: "Will all passengers please stay in their seats and fasten their seat belts." I looked out of the window again. We were still in thick black cloud. Then the rain started. Suddenly there was a flash of lightning.

It was very near, but I was not afraid. "It's only a storm," I thought. Then the plane jumped again and started to roll from side to side. I saw the lights in the front: "No smoking. Fasten seat belts." The plane started to spin. I heard thunder. I heard terrible screams. There was another flash of lightning. Suddenly the sky was full of lightning. No, it was full of flames. A bright yellow flame flashed out of the right wing of the plane. I heard my mother's quiet voice: "This is the end," she said.

Then I heard a loud BANG.

I was wet and cold. Where was I? I could still feel my seat belt. I was still in my seat, but I wasn't in the plane. I was in the air. I looked down. I could see the jungle very clearly. I could see the dark green treetops. They started to spin towards me. Then they came towards me very fast. I shut my eyes and held tightly onto my seat...

Suddenly there was a flash of lightning.

The treetops started to spin towards me.

Suzanne's father waited for his wife and daughter. He waited all day. He did some work in the morning and then had lunch. In the afternoon he tried to read. After tea he put the presents for his family under the Christmas tree. Night came so he lit a lamp. He looked at his watch. The plane was very late. Pépé started to sing. "Hello, Suzanne. Hello. Happy Christmas. Happy Christmas."

He smiled at the bird.

"She'll be here soon," he said. He looked at his watch again. It was eight o'clock so he turned on the radio. He sat close to the loudspeaker and listened carefully to the news. He heard a man's voice:

"This is the news. There have been terrible storms today. The 07.30 plane from Lima to Pucallpa took off late this morning. It crashed in the jungle this afternoon. There were 80 passengers on the plane. We are looking for the plane but we do not know…"

The sound was very weak so he couldn't hear the man's voice clearly. He turned the radio off and Pépé started to sing again.

"Hello, Suzanne. Happy Christmas."

"I'm sorry, Pépé," he said. "She's not coming home tonight. Go to sleep now."

Sadly he sat beside the Christmas tree and thought about his wife and daughter. In the end he went to bed, but he couldn't sleep.

I opened my eyes and saw my seat from the plane.

The rain hit my face. "Wake up! Wake up!" it said. I heard thunder in my strange dreams. No, it was real thunder. I was still in a storm but I was on the ground. I was very wet and very cold. I opened my eyes and saw my seat from the plane. I saw my mother's seat, too, but I couldn't see her. I couldn't see very clearly. Where were my glasses? I put my hands up to my face. My glasses weren't there. One eye hurt and there was a strange lump on my head. I looked down at my feet. I only had one shoe on. My left foot was bare and there was a very nasty cut on it. Suddenly the storm stopped.

"I must get up and find my mother," I thought. But I couldn't get up. The lump on my head and the cut on my foot didn't hurt but I was very tired. And I felt weak. I could see the thick trees of the jungle and I could hear the sounds of the jungle. Birds sang and insects buzzed. I was in the jungle and it was still day. I knew the jungle, so I was not afraid. I'm only afraid of large cities. I lay under the seat and tried to think. "Where is my mother? Whcre are the other passengers? Where is the plane?" But my head felt strange and I couldn't think clearly. I listened to the birds and the insects. Night came suddenly. It always does in the jungle. Then I heard the frogs. The birds go to sleep at night but the frogs croak all night. I like that sound, so I soon fell asleep.

The frogs
croak all night.

I woke up early the next morning and got up, but I still felt strange. I couldn't see straight. I looked at the trees and they moved. Then they started to spin. I sat down on the ground again, and shut my eyes. The ground didn't move under me. Slowly I opened my eyes and looked round me. Suddenly I saw a little parcel. I picked it up and opened it. I found a bag of sweets and a Christmas cake inside the parcel. Then I remembered.

"It's Christmas Day," I thought. "It's Christmas Day and I'm in the jungle. The plane crashed, but I'm still alive."

I found a bag of sweets inside the parcel.

Rivers are the roads
of the jungle.

I thought about my home and my parents.

"Dad's waiting for us at home," I thought. "He has found a Christmas tree and he's sitting beside it. Perhaps he's talking to Pépé? Has Pépé learned some new words? Mummy said… Where is my mother?" I looked at the empty seat from the plane. "Is she still alive? Is she near here? Perhaps she is hurt. I must find her." Then I thought sadly, "Perhaps she died in the crash, and I'll never see her again. What will my father do?" I thought of my father, my kind, clever father.

"I must find the way home. My father will need me. Perhaps he has lost his wife. He mustn't lose his daughter, too."

Then I heard his voice in my head.

"Find a river, Suzanne. Find a river. Rivers are the roads of the jungle. Find a river."

Suddenly I felt better.

a snake
(*boa constrictor*)

mosquitoes

a spider
(*tarantula*)

I got up and found a stick. You must always carry a stick in the jungle. Hold the stick in front of you. Poke it into the undergrowth – the tree roots and the creepers. Poke it into all the thick plants and low bushes in front of you. Then the snakes and insects will bite the stick and run away. They won't bite you. I knew the rules of the jungle well. My parents are clever scientists and they have lived in the jungle for many years. They taught me the rules of the jungle.

"Don't be afraid of the large animals, Suzanne. They're afraid of you. But the small ones are dangerous, the snakes and the insects: the flies, mosquitoes, ants and spiders. They can kill you, but follow the rules and you'll be safe. Carry a stick. Make a noise. Don't stop. Don't eat strange fruit. Find a river. Always follow a river. People live near rivers."

I felt hungry so I tasted the Christmas cake. It was very wet and I couldn't eat it. So I threw the cake away and opened the bag of sweets. I sucked one slowly. That parcel was my Christmas present from the jungle. I was lucky. I was alive and I had a Christmas present – some sweets. I held my stick tightly and started to walk.

I took four or five steps but the world started to spin again. I stopped and rested for a short time. Then I tried to go on. My head felt very strange so I stopped again.

"What am I going to do?" I thought. "I must find a river. I must not stop."

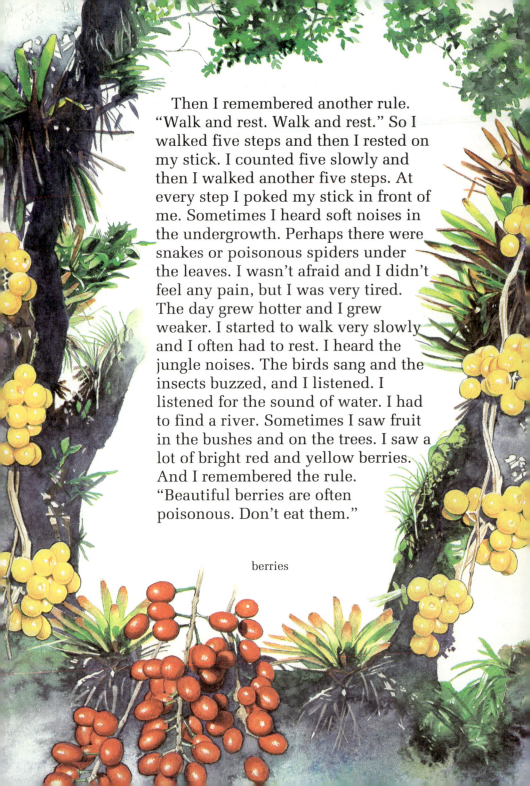

Then I remembered another rule. "Walk and rest. Walk and rest." So I walked five steps and then I rested on my stick. I counted five slowly and then I walked another five steps. At every step I poked my stick in front of me. Sometimes I heard soft noises in the undergrowth. Perhaps there were snakes or poisonous spiders under the leaves. I wasn't afraid and I didn't feel any pain, but I was very tired. The day grew hotter and I grew weaker. I started to walk very slowly and I often had to rest. I heard the jungle noises. The birds sang and the insects buzzed, and I listened. I listened for the sound of water. I had to find a river. Sometimes I saw fruit in the bushes and on the trees. I saw a lot of bright red and yellow berries. And I remembered the rule. "Beautiful berries are often poisonous. Don't eat them."

berries

I sucked another sweet and began to feel better. I started to walk quite quickly. Then I heard a new sound, the best sound in the world. I heard the sound of water. And it was quite near. I struggled through the creepers and bushes with my stick. I hurried towards the sound of the water. Towards the river. The sound was very near and the ground was quite soft under my feet. I took a big step between two trees and there it was – water. But it wasn't a river. It was only a little stream.

"Oh no," I thought. "This isn't the way home."

Sadly I sat down on the bank and looked at the little stream. The water ran fast and it was very clear.

"It's clean water," I thought. "I can drink it." Then I remembered the old saying: "Large rivers grow from small streams."

"That's right," I thought. "I'll follow this stream. It will take me to a bigger stream. And in the end it will take me to a river, a real river."

So I had a drink and washed my face. I looked at my left foot. The cut was quite big (5 cm deep and 2 cm wide). I tried to wash off the dry blood but new blood started to flow. I remembered the piranhas. Piranhas are little fish with very sharp teeth. They can always smell blood and they swim very fast. Hundreds of them attack you and bite off your flesh. They kill you very quickly…

Piranhas are little fish
with very sharp teeth.

15

You step on an alligator and then its large cruel mouth shuts – snap.

Alligators can smell blood, too and they have a lot of sharp teeth. They lie on the banks of rivers and wait. They often look like old tree trunks so people don't see them. You step on an alligator and then its large cruel mouth shuts – snap. I didn't want to be an alligator's dinner or food for the piranhas. There was new blood on my foot, but I had to stay near the stream. I had to follow the little stream to a river. It was a dangerous road, but it was a road.

I started to walk again. Every step was a struggle. The bank was thick with roots and creepers. Sometimes big tree trunks stopped me. I tried to find a way round them but I often had to walk in the stream. Then my feet stuck in the soft sand at the bottom of the stream. I grew very tired. It was late afternoon and the sun grew hotter and hotter. My head began to buzz – zz – zz and I couldn't see clearly. The buzz grew louder and louder. It filled my head, but it wasn't in my head. It was a real noise. Flies, hundreds of flies – buzz –. Then I saw it. A seat from the plane. There were three dead bodies on the seat. They were black with flies and dry blood. Dead bodies are food for flies and flies are always hungry. Buzz – buzz – I felt sick and my eyes filled with tears. Was one of the bodies my mother? I had to look. No. It was three girls. I walked away.

"I'm a lucky girl," I thought. "I'm still alive. Now I must find the way home."

I walked and walked. The stream didn't flow straight, so I couldn't walk straight. But I knew the rules. I must follow the stream. I mustn't stop. Suddenly the sun dropped from the sky and night came. I had to find a safe place for the night. I found shelter under some trees on the bank and lay down. I rested but I didn't sleep well. All night I heard danger.

"What are those strange noises in the bushes?" I thought. "Snakes? Or alligators? Or a hungry jaguar?" I felt an insect on my bare leg. It crawled up and up. I didn't move. Perhaps it was a poisonous spider. Then it crawled away, but I still couldn't sleep. Once I heard a terrible scream. Was it a person or a monkey? Jaguars hunt at night. They kill monkeys and eat them. Sometimes they kill people, too. I tried to forget the dangers. I tried to think about nice things. I thought about my father and Pépé. I thought about our safe little home in the jungle. Then the mosquitoes found me. Buzz – buzz – bite – buzz – bite – all night.

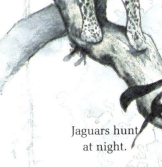

Jaguars hunt at night.

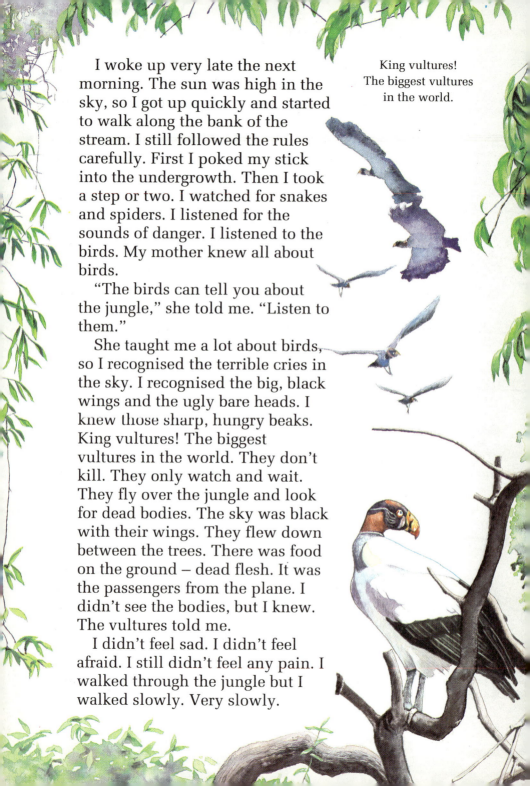

I woke up very late the next morning. The sun was high in the sky, so I got up quickly and started to walk along the bank of the stream. I still followed the rules carefully. First I poked my stick into the undergrowth. Then I took a step or two. I watched for snakes and spiders. I listened for the sounds of danger. I listened to the birds. My mother knew all about birds.

"The birds can tell you about the jungle," she told me. "Listen to them."

She taught me a lot about birds, so I recognised the terrible cries in the sky. I recognised the big, black wings and the ugly bare heads. I knew those sharp, hungry beaks. King vultures! The biggest vultures in the world. They don't kill. They only watch and wait. They fly over the jungle and look for dead bodies. The sky was black with their wings. They flew down between the trees. There was food on the ground – dead flesh. It was the passengers from the plane. I didn't see the bodies, but I knew. The vultures told me.

I didn't feel sad. I didn't feel afraid. I still didn't feel any pain. I walked through the jungle but I walked slowly. Very slowly.

King vultures!
The biggest vultures
in the world.

I passed some pieces of the plane. I saw the number clearly on one piece of metal: OBR 941. I saw other passengers' cases. I could smell dead bodies. I could hear the hungry vultures. But I couldn't hear people's voices. I couldn't see any people. I was afraid. "Are all the other passengers dead?" I thought. "Am I alone in the jungle?"

The second day ended and night came. I slept quite well, but on the third day in the jungle I started to feel pain. The lump on my head hurt, my foot hurt, and the sun burnt my back. I couldn't fasten my dress at the back, so the sun shone through the trees onto my bare skin. The hot sun burnt my back and the cruel flies and mosquitoes attacked me. But I was stronger on the third day. I had some sweets and there was clear water in the stream. I went on. Stick – foot – stick – foot. The flies and mosquitoes buzzed round me and stung me. I tried to brush them off my face and arms but I couldn't. There were hundreds of them, and my arm grew tired. They were very large flies, and their stings hurt me terribly. I tried to think about other things. I tried to forget the pain.

Suddenly I heard a new sound, the best sound in the world. Planes! I heard planes in the sky. I forgot the flies and shouted:

"Hello! Help! Hello!"

But they couldn't see me and they couldn't hear me. I was under the thick, green trees. I couldn't see the planes. I could only hear them.

"Help!" I shouted. "Help! Hello!" Slowly the noise died away and I was alone again. But I was happier. I could walk. I wasn't hungry. I could drink from the clear stream. There was still hope.

"Perhaps they will come back tomorrow," I thought.

That afternoon it grew very hot and I often had to rest. There were a lot of storms. There was thunder and lightning, and heavy, jungle rain. I wasn't afraid of the storms. I was safe on the ground, but I was soon terribly wet.

Then the rain stopped and I saw a thick line of ants in front of me. They looked like a big, black snake, but I recognised them. They were very dangerous ants. They march through the jungle and attack all the insects in their path. They attack small animals, too. The Indians are afraid of these ants. Hundreds of them march through their villages and eat their food. Sometimes they sting the babies asleep in the huts. "They're marching straight towards *me*," I thought, "and there's still blood on my foot."

I jumped quickly into the stream. The water was quite deep but I was already wet. The water came up to the top of my legs so I could only walk very slowly. Another storm came. I tried to shelter under the trees, but the rain still came through. It fell down like a river from the sky. I couldn't see through it. I just held my stick tightly and struggled on. Suddenly the rain stopped and I saw a bigger river in front of me. I felt new hope. This was a better road.

I saw a thick line of ants in front of me.

I moved onto the bank of the new river. I was hungry but I couldn't find any sweets in the bag. Why? I felt inside the bag again and found… a big hole.

"All the sweets have gone," I thought, "so now I haven't got any food. But I can still drink, so I can still walk."

I moved slowly and painfully along the bank. I could see alligators in the big river and they could see me. They started to swim towards me. I could see their ugly mouths full of sharp teeth. I tried to hurry, but I had to walk carefully. I had to watch the ground in front of me. I had to watch for snakes, spiders, ants, and alligators. The flies and the mosquitoes were always there. They never stopped. Buzz – buzz – bite – buzz – buzz. The flies were the worst. They stung me again and again. Then I remembered about the flies. They lay their eggs under your skin. You must get them out quickly. The eggs grow into terrible maggots, and the maggots eat your flesh.

"I must go on," I thought. "I must find help. I must find people. Where are all the Indians?"

I tried to shelter under the trees.

I saw birds and butterflies. I saw beautiful flowers and bright berries. I saw lots of animals. Monkeys played in the trees or ran along the bank in front of me. They played happily and didn't run away. Then I knew. There weren't any Indians near us. The Indians hunt monkeys, so the monkeys are afraid of them. Monkeys don't go near Indian villages. But these monkeys weren't afraid of people. They didn't run away from me.

For the first time since the crash I was really afraid. The pain in my arms grew worse and I saw baby maggots under the skin. "The flies' eggs are starting to grow," I thought. "I must get them out."

I started to hear strange noises. One day I heard chickens. "That's lucky," I thought. "I'll soon find people and some food." But it wasn't a chicken. It was a strange jungle bird. I knew all the birds near my home, but I didn't recognise that bird. Then I knew. I was miles from my home.

a butterfly

Monkeys played
in the trees.

One morning I heard another plane, but it was high up in the clouds. It couldn't see me, so it couldn't help me. "Where can I find help?" I thought. "Where?"

I had to rest so I lay down on the sand. I shut my eyes and tried to sleep, but I heard another strange noise. I looked behind me. Then I saw them. Five baby alligators lay close behind me. They were very small. They couldn't hurt me, but their parents could.

"Get up, Suzanne," I said. "Move on. You can't go to sleep next to an alligator family."

I walked and walked. Stick – step – rest – stick – step – rest. Day followed night and night followed day. When did I get the maggots out of my arms and legs? Was it on the fourth day or the fifth? I had a metal ring on one finger. I took this ring off and broke it. Then I made a knife from it and dug out the maggots.

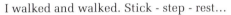

I walked and walked. Stick - step - rest...

"I must kill them all," I thought, "or they will kill me." But other flies came and laid their eggs in the holes. I poked into my arms with my 'knife' and dug the new maggots out. It hurt but it helped. "These maggots will *not* eat me," I thought. "*I'm* going to kill *them* first!" I started to hear voices in my head. I heard Pépé. I heard my parents. My father said: "Swim, Suzanne. You must learn to swim. Perhaps one day you will need to swim. Swim, swim."

Yes, I could swim. I could swim in the big river, but then I remembered the piranhas. There was still blood on my foot and on my arms. I looked into the water. It was clear. I couldn't see any fish or any alligators. I jumped in and started to swim. But there were tree trunks across the river. There were branches of trees. There were rapids. Did I swim? Did the river carry me? I can't remember. I was in a dream, a terrible dream. In the end I came to some dangerous rapids and climbed back onto the bank.

I came to some dangerous rapids and climbed back onto the bank.

I started to walk along the bank but the trees grew very close to the river. Their branches often hit my face. I remembered the fire ants. They drop down from the trees and sting you. All the time I had to watch for danger. The jungle is beautiful, but it can kill you. The birds sang, "Kill you, kill you, kill you." I didn't want to hear them. I only wanted to sleep. I wanted to sleep for days. I shut my eyes and took another step. Suddenly a bird cried out. I heard my mother's voice.

"Listen to the birds, Suzanne. Always listen to the birds. They will tell you about the jungle."

The bird cried again. "Danger, danger."

I opened my eyes. There was a large snake on a branch in front of me. I started to scream but my voice stuck in my throat. I couldn't move. Then I saw – the snake was asleep. Slowly and very quietly I walked round the tree. I found a clear piece of ground and lay down. I didn't try to dig out any maggots. I didn't drink. I could only lie there.

"I want to sleep," I thought. "I can't go on. I must sleep. Sleep will end the pain. Sleep."

I started to scream but my voice stuck in my throat.

In his home near Pucallpa Suzanne's father tried to work. He was alone. His wife and daughter were dead so he only had his work. It was eight days since the crash. Men flew over the jungle for three days but they didn't find the plane.

Suzanne's father tried to work.

People can't live in the jungle after a plane crash. They haven't got the right clothes or food. They haven't got knives or shelter. Suddenly he remembered an American boy. Perhaps there was still hope? That boy lost his way in the jungle but stayed alive for a week. He found a river and followed it to Pucallpa. Suzanne's mother nursed the American boy. She was a good nurse and a very clever scientist, too. She knew all about birds. She rescued Pépé from the jungle and mended his broken wing. Then she and Suzanne taught him to talk.

Suzanne's mother mended Pépé's broken wing.

He looked round the room. Pépé was very quiet. What was wrong? Pépé lay on the top of the radio and didn't move. Pépé was dead.

I dreamed about the American boy. He came to our home in the jungle. He lost his way but then he found a river. The river rescued him and he lived. My parents found him and nursed him. My mother spoke to me in my dreams. "He did it, Suzanne. *You* can do it, too. Your father needs you, Suzanne."

I woke up. I must go on. Follow the river. The rain fell heavily all day and the river flowed very fast. My left eye was very swollen and my arms and legs were swollen, too. I stopped and tried to dig out some maggots but the sun burnt my bare back. I jumped into the river and swam down it for some time. The fast water washed out some maggots and took the pain from my arms. Another storm came and the river started to run very fast. It was dangerous so I crawled back onto the bank and looked for food. Big, black frogs jumped up in front of me.

"You can eat frogs," I thought, "but first you must catch one." The frogs croaked, "You can't catch us. You can't."

I was very tired and very weak. I couldn't catch those quick frogs so I didn't try. Then the rain stopped and the sun came out again. It grew hotter. "I must walk all day," I thought. "I must only rest at night, but I need rest now."

Rest from danger, rest from pain.

I had to lie down, so I looked for a safe place.

Then I saw it. There was a boat, a real boat in the river. I went close to it. It was a small, new boat.

"Some hunters have come here," I thought. "They came here by boat and they've fastened it to the bank. They'll come back, but where have they gone?"

I looked behind me and saw a little path through the bushes. Then, at the end of the path, I saw a little hut. I hurried towards the hut. It was new, too. I went inside. The hut was dark and cool, and there was a plastic sheet on the clean floor.

"I'll sleep here tonight," I thought. "It's cool and safe, so I'll sleep well."

But I couldn't sleep. I listened for voices. I looked out of the little door for lights. Suddenly I saw a fire. The flames danced in front of the door. I looked again. It was only fireflies. In the end I took the plastic sheet and went back to the river bank, near the boat. I crawled under the plastic sheet. It sheltered me from the mosquitoes, but I still couldn't sleep. The pain in my arms was terrible and I could hear dangerous noises. But early in the morning I did sleep for an hour or two. The next day I felt better.

Then, at the end of the path, I saw a little hut.

28

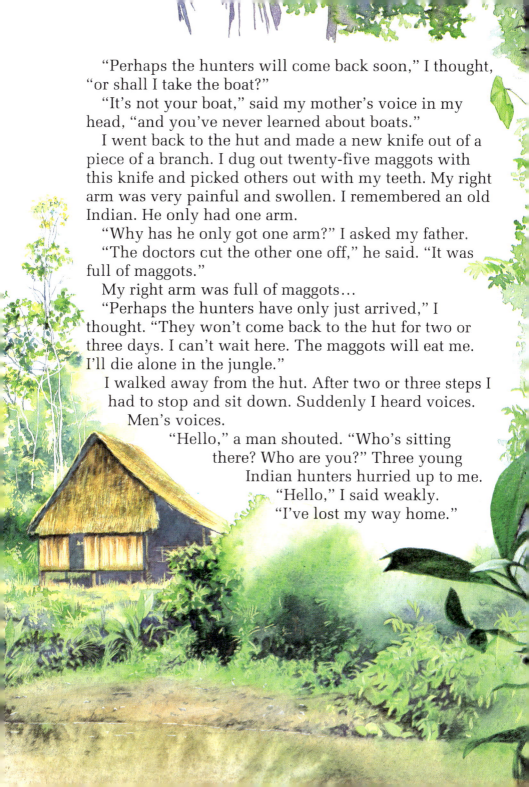

"Perhaps the hunters will come back soon," I thought, "or shall I take the boat?"

"It's not your boat," said my mother's voice in my head, "and you've never learned about boats."

I went back to the hut and made a new knife out of a piece of a branch. I dug out twenty-five maggots with this knife and picked others out with my teeth. My right arm was very painful and swollen. I remembered an old Indian. He only had one arm.

"Why has he only got one arm?" I asked my father.

"The doctors cut the other one off," he said. "It was full of maggots."

My right arm was full of maggots…

"Perhaps the hunters have only just arrived," I thought. "They won't come back to the hut for two or three days. I can't wait here. The maggots will eat me. I'll die alone in the jungle."

I walked away from the hut. After two or three steps I had to stop and sit down. Suddenly I heard voices. Men's voices.

"Hello," a man shouted. "Who's sitting there? Who are you?" Three young Indian hunters hurried up to me.

"Hello," I said weakly. "I've lost my way home."

One man spoke. "Tell us. Who are you? Where's your home? You're very sick. We must take you home."

"I was in a plane," I said. "It crashed on Christmas Eve. I fell from the sky and now I'm trying to find Pucallpa. My father is waiting for me."

"Young woman," said the man, "that was a terrible crash. All the passengers are dead. We heard the news on the radio. That was on Christmas Day. Have you been alone in the jungle for ten days?"

Ten days. Was it ten days?

"But can't you see," I said. "I'm *alive*!" They laughed then, and I laughed with them. But we didn't laugh much. I was very sick and we all knew it.

I sat between the hunters in their little boat.

"Come on," said the hunters. "We must find a doctor." They picked me up and carried me to the hut. They took a clean, metal knife and dug a lot of fat maggots out of my flesh. They washed me and gave me some food. But I wasn't hungry and couldn't eat much. Then they took me to the boat. I sat between the hunters in their little boat. I was very weak and very tired, but I felt happy.

"I'm safe now," I thought. "I'm not alone against the jungle."

30

I lay between cool white sheets. My head felt better and I still had my right arm. The door opened and the doctor came in.

"How are you today?" he asked.

"I feel very well," I said. "Can I go home?"

He smiled. "You must wait another week. You've been very ill. The jungle nearly killed you. You don't want to go back to the jungle."

"But I do," I cried. "I love the jungle. My home's in the jungle. I must go home. My father's waiting for me."

"Wait a minute," said the doctor. "You have a visitor." He went to the door and called, "She's just woken up. You can come in."

My father came into the room.

"Suzanne," he said. "Oh, Suzanne."

I couldn't speak. Then I said, "Father, I'm sorry. Mummy was next to me in the plane, but..." I felt tears in my eyes.

"I know," he said, "I know. But *you're* still alive."

"I want to come home," I said. "I want to see Pépé." My father looked at the doctor. There were tears in his eyes.

"I'm sorry, Suzanne," he said. "Pépé... Pépé is dead."

Pépé, my little bird. Pépé was a present from my mother. She rescued him and mended his wing. We taught him to talk. "My mother really is dead," I thought and my eyes filled with tears. "And our little Pépé is dead, too."

For the first time since the crash I started to cry.

# READING ACTIVITIES

## Before reading

1 This story is about a girl in the jungle. What do you know about jungles? Look at the pictures. How many animals, insects, birds and plants can you find?

2 How can you find your way in a large city? What are the dangers in a large city? What are the dangers in the jungle?

## While reading

1 Write a newspaper report about the crash, with the headline: "Christmas plane crashes in jungle". Use the radio report on page 8 to help you, but remember to change "this morning" to "yesterday morning" etc.

2 Decide if the following sentences are *true* or *false*. If *false*, rewrite with the correct information.
a) Suzanne found her mother.
b) She ate all of the Christmas cake.
c) The flies and the mosquitoes didn't sting Suzanne.
d) The ants laid their eggs under Suzanne's skin.
e) After five days Suzanne found a small boat.

3 Answer these questions about the story.
a) Why did Suzanne try to find a river?
b) Why did she always carry a stick?
c) Why was she afraid to swim in the river?
d) Why didn't the planes see Suzanne?
e) Why didn't the monkeys run away from Suzanne? What did that tell her?

## After reading

1 Now complete your list of animals, insects, birds and plants. Which are dangerous? Which are beautiful? Which are both?

2 List the rules Suzanne followed to stay alive in the jungle.

3 The Indians took Suzanne to a village to see a doctor. When her father arrived, what questions did he ask the doctor and what did the doctor tell him? Write the dialogue.

Material devised by Monica Vincent and Anne Collins.